Basic information

Electrical Engineering Concepts

Creating your own iot device

Creating your own iot device in arduino

M2M,IOT things introduction

In the ancient china, a man came to an emperor with his invention of chess, he demonstrated it to his king, and king was very impressed with his invention and asked him what he expects as a reward. The man told the king, he wants grain of rice to be placed on square doubling the grain rice on each subsequent square.

King thought it to be very humble and modest reward and asked his servant to fulfill the request, by the time the rice grains filled the first half of the chessboard, he had more than 4 billion rice grains, by the time the servant got to 64th square, the man had more than ($18x10^{18}$) or more than all the wealth of the land.

If you ask me, how much is the growth potential for IOT (Internet of Things). It is exponential, as new devices get designed, more objects become m2m more the growth potential is.

Since you are reading my eBook, I assume that you are a student who wants to learn about IOT, so I will be sharing links to the course of IOT and the material where you can purchase devices to make your IOT device, implementing the IOT concepts will enhance your understanding about IOT.

Web 1.0 allowed humans to read content from web pages, web 1.0 is the first generation of web, web2.0 is the second generation where browsers can well be client as well as server, pushing & receiving data from the client to the server, in web 1.0 browser use to connect to the server take data and then disconnect from the server, but in web 2.0 browser maintains continuous connection with the server pushing & receiving data back and forth, take example of gmail.com, facebook.com

But in web 3.0 machines can read and understand data just like humans, it is internet of things or m2m(machine to machine communication), devices have capability to sense and communicate with other things

ebook is divided into 3 parts, to build your tempo, direct explanation of technical details will bore your so iam explaining it step by step first it gives information about things which are already in market regarding iot, career opportunities and how you can benefit from it.

to build iot apps, you need to be a programmer and also electrical engineer, basic electrical knowledge will do

to actually build iot devices, you will need understanding of maths, electrical engineering and computer programming, and understanding of boards, your hardware device limitations, the process will start from the idea and then prototyping and then actual manufacturing.

if your product is good and you think it is useful that people will actually pay for it, you can get funding and mass produce in china, almost all iot devices are made in china.

Shenzhen is the iot devices manufacturing hub in china.

there is a new 3D printer coming up, "MakerArm", it can print circuit boards for you, that printer is currently available for preorder on kickstarter.

book is designed in such a way, that even non-technical person understands it and does not fall asleep while reading it.

Benefits of IOT

A device which is not connected to the internet is a dumb device. IOT device can improve usefulness and save costs.

IOT is beneficial in Health care, Transportation, Automating tasks, understanding patterns, Tracking behavior for real-time marketing, Enhanced situational awareness, Sensor-driven decision analytics, Process optimization, Optimized resource consumption, Instantaneous control and response in complex autonomous systems

- Ubiquitous networks – personal wi-fi on your mobile phone and on every other device. Everyone (and everything) wants and needs to be connected.

- Connected computing – we want all of our devices, phones, televisions, music players, vehicles, etc. to keep track of what we are doing, viewing, reading, and listening to as we move through our day, from place to place – the handoffs from device to device are already happening.

- Ubiquitous sensors – on everything. It is already here – the Internet of Everything and the wearables revolution.

- Intelligence at the periphery of the network – Jim Gray, the visionary database guru from Microsoft, envisioned smart sensors acting as a mini-database with embedded machine learning algorithms. Here is how he said it (10 years ago): "Intelligence is moving to the periphery of the network. Each disk and each sensor will be a competent database machine."

- Analytics-as-a-Service – the API and App economies are already vast and growing – this enables any "thing" to "do something interesting" as long as it can connect to an API or invoke an App that performs a network-based service. The "thing" is a data generator and/or collector that also learns from, makes predictions, and maybe even takes data-driven actions in response to the data that are collected (through the versatility and convenience of an App or API call).

- Marketing automation – mobile customer engagement, geolocation, Apple's iBeacon, etc. are all creating a network of knowledge about customers' locations, intentions, preferences, and buying patterns. Of course, this degree of location-based knowledge needs to strike the right balance between user privacy and the timely delivery of useful products and services to that user.

- Supply Chain Analytics – delivering just-in-time products at the point of need (including the use of RFID-based tracking). Essentially, everything is a customer (including machines, automobiles, manufacturing plants, ATM machines, etc.), and the IoT is monitoring, watching, and waiting for a product need to arise.

- Aging workforce! Really? – Yes! There is a huge hiring gap in manufacturing, which is pushing toward more automation, robotics, M2M (Machine-to-Machine), machine log mining, 3-D printing, predictive and prescriptive analytics in the machines that are doing that work for us. As the classic rock song "2525" predicted would happen in the year 5555: "some machine is doing that for you."

- Transportation: We have been using GPS to track movement of delivery trucks for years. IOT eases and simplifies the entire process by introducing a monetary sensor that helps to track distance and time locations and other contributing factors.

- Inventory management: As managing fleet, inventory management and tracking is also a major task. IOT is used to tag radio frequency sensors to track the location of products in real time. It has been instrumental in tracking the level of inventory and to stock it in advance, making alerts for unforeseen stoppages, automatically placing orders, etc.

- Promotions: Many businesses use IOT to send mobile promotions to frequent shoppers. This is done by keeping track of the shoppers history and shopping interests. It utilizes location-based tracking of the physical shoppers as well as those shopping over the internet.

- Assessing web user intelligence: IOT is used by third party web data aggregators to have a better understanding of their customer by tracking them on social media networks. This is essential to identify the key customers and their preferences.

- Facilitates warranty and maintenance services: IOT enables product tracking. This in turn helps to keep a track of products that require maintenance or warranty. This also helps in crisis moments like thefts to track and place a product.

- Vending technology: IOT has played a big role in enhancing the working of vending machines by enabling them to communicate to monitor inventory levels, determine pricing, etc.

While this chapter highlights some key benefits of IOT, in the next chapter I have explained the terms like RFID and AR markers because they are important to the concept of IOT, especially RFID.

Some of the communication protocols for iot

- Http
- Xbee
- MQTT
- BLE
- RFID

some new protocols came up, designed specifically for iot devices to be more efficient.

Http

this is the basic protocol, where we pass data as a json via url to the cloud server or any of our web server.

Xbee

Xbee is the wireless microcontroller made by Digi International, it uses zigbee protocol, it is basically communication between 2 wireless radios.

it consists of 3 pins and an antenna, it has 11 digital pins and 4 analog pins, iam pasting the image below, how it looks like

MQTT

it is better than http for iot devices, mqtt is more designed for iot devices, http requires more bandwidth and much more battery power, which is inefficient for small iot devices, mqtt is much like meteor framework programming model, subscribe publish model, communication is in binary format, so less bandwidth, lightweight and consumes less battery power.

https://mosquitto.org/

you can download open source program for it from the website, and run it as a broker, any clients which are connected to particular topic will receive messages, if there are any new messages on that particular topic.

Ble

it is wireless network technology based on bluetooth protocol, but it requires lot less energy, major adopters of ble technology is health and fitness devices and apps.

RFID

For developing IOT devices, we must understand RFID (Radio Frequency Identification) as well, RFID is barcode in chip format, information on chip can be updated as well, and is capable of communicating with RFID reading enabled other devices, as the prices are getting RFID chips are getting lower and lower every day, its use is only going to increase.

RFID provides unique identification for an object, without RFID there would be no way for wireless networks to identify each other, currently it's used in many devices like mobile phones, tablets, computers, credit cards, access cards, and many other things

What is AR Markers

Ar Markers (Augmented Reality) Marker is effectively two dimensional symbols, similar to a QR code that allows a camera to determine position and rotation relative to a surface. With this information, a camera can do many different things.

It is used in video games, when you scan AR marker with your mobile camera, an animated character will come out of it

You can check this YouTube video

https://www.youtube.com/watch?v=PTK_qfh2fD8

or search in YouTube for AR Markers

You will get several demo videos

Industrial Internet of things

Factories can automate their repeated tasks, which can both improve productivity and efficiency,
a simple case study, an IOT consultant is invited to a mid-size potato chip company, to figure out the inefficiency and ways to automate things and to improve productivity and efficiency.

after the chips are baked they move along a conveyor belt where a team of workers wait to inspect them, looking for either overcooked or undercooked chips, when team spots an unacceptable chip, he will just flip the chip on the floor, and the belt will move on, later that chips which are thrown on floor are collected and included in feed for farm animals, you can easily see here a team of people watching chips moving on the conveyor belt whole day and flipping chips which are unacceptable, it is also error prone and the job is of course very boring, here the automation can take place and remove inefficiency and improve productivity.

A simple webcam over the top of the conveyor belt and special computer vision software which can detect bad chips and strategically placed air nozzles would shoot tiny puffs of air at the chips in question blowing them off the belt.

This type of solution is already implemented in many potato chips company, it also saves money and improves efficiency, and staff which is employed to flip the bad chips can now be utilized in other area, where it can bring more efficiency or sales.

If you are planning to be an IOT consultant this could be the job for you, automate the industries bring down their costs, improve efficiency and automate as much as possible to boost productivity

Machines have tendency to break down due to variety of reason, a mechanic is always present in the assembly line, just in case a problem occurs, we can free him or lessen his work, by using IOT solution to the machines,

IOT solutions can monitor the machines using webcam and detect vibrations, when vibrations exceed a certain level, that means conveyor belt or gears are slipping , or some other issue, if the vibrations has altogether stopped that means machine has halted production, now mechanics can be alerted

IOT enabled machines can detect overheating and slow down its production, IOT enabled machines can detect occurrence of problem, with this data we can better understand machines and manage accordingly, we can predict future failures and act accordingly.

Consumer IOT

You must heard & seen on Tv, that how a 12th pass student has made an app, which can track your motorbike location, preventing it from getting stolen, this are actually very simple IOT devices which anyone who can read and write can make, there are tutorials available for that.

I am putting list of successful IOT products

Fitbit

fitbit develops IOT devices to monitor your health, fitbit is an physical activity tracker designed to help people became more active, basically help people become healthier human being, it was introduced by its co founder Eric Friedman & James Park in 2008, in short it's a 21st century pedometer

The product is deceptively simple, its only 2 inches long and 1.2 inches thick, throughout the day

You can check more about it in YouTube

https://www.youtube.com/watch?v=93s1EsgdowA

Search in YouTube for Fitbit to understand it more

Amazon Echo

Amazon echo is amazing IOT device, round shaped speaker, which is always connected to the internet, and whenever you say "Alexa" it gets activated and will listen to your command.

For ex. "Alexa What Time is it", it will tell your current time, it will tell time according to your current location.

It can play music for you, it can read news for you, it will answer most of your question, and it can help kids do homework.

Amazon Echo can Read Kindle Books for you, can play audible books, it can also be your alarm clock and wake you up on time you set.

Amazon Echo can be connected to your home devices, and then you can switch lights on or off

Amazon Echo can take down your shopping orders and directly shop from amazon, It is far better than Apple Siri.

I just wanted to introduce you to amazon echo, you can Google about amazon echo, and YouTube it to get to know more about amazon echo

Check out more about it in YouTube

https://www.youtube.com/watch?v=KkOCeAtKHlc

Jibo

This is similar to amazon echo, but it is lot better since it has face, this is lot better than amazon echo, but since a big company like Amazon is behind Echo it is selling more.

https://www.youtube.com/watch?v=3N1Q8oFpX1Y

It is also an IOT enabled speaking device (Assistant), you will never feel lonely if you have JIBO

Amazon Dash

You never run low on things which are important to you, it's amazon dash button available to amazon prime members, whenever you are low on particular day to day consumer product you just need to press the dash button and it will order it for you.

There are 18 different brand buttons currently available, each button is decorated with the brand logo and you can keep it anywhere, whenever it gets low you just press the button. It's a very simple IOT device.

Check out this amazon dash video
https://www.youtube.com/watch?v=EHMXXOB6qPA

Amazon is bringing many new changes in consumer service, it's making new radical innovation, I think it will overtake Google, since Google is busy with DARPA, amazon will run over Google in consumer related products.

Amazon is also working on better version of "Amazon Dash", "Amazon Dash Replenishment", it will monitor and analyze your use of a particular product and will auto order it for you, so you don't fall short on the product you use the most. This will make life very easy for you, since you won't have to remember small things.

https://www.youtube.com/watch?v=vTYcWG6BIDY

What they are trying to do is to take humans off from ordering cycle

Amazon is simply amazing in doing day to day innovations for use of common people.

IFFT
(If this then that) is a cool, IOT enabled service

If helps you connect all your apps, you can also connect your IOT Devices like fitbit, you can connect your home lights with IFFT, like IFFT can blink your home lights if someone photo tags you on facebook, there are many recipes available, you can also create your own recipes

Learn more about it

https://ifttt.com/

If you are very busy person, this thing can help you save time, you can automate things.

Philips Hue

If it basically allows you to control your light bulbs from anywhere, it's an IOT enabled light bulbs system. You can even program with ifttt.com to blink, whenever some 1 tags you in photo. You can even make it to change light colors with your favorite music to enhance your mood, if you configure it with amazon echo or Apple Siri you can switch lights on and off with your words.

Check its YouTube video demo

https://www.youtube.com/watch?v=h1falu7l8bg

Success Stories in IOT

Intelligent waste management (Burba Project)

EU had set goals to for waste separation and recycling but it was not able to achieve it, the goal had to be viable economically and environmentally

Problems with the company side

The waste collection is routinely scheduled and cannot be adjusted when there is spike in waste

sorting of waste difficult as citizens mix up the waste

feed of waste reaching recycling unit is not efficient

routine pick up of trucks is not optimized

Best location of street garbage containers to minimize costs is difficult to estimate since lack of qualitative and quantitative data

containers many a times displaced by by-passers for car parking or by vandals

Problems with Citizen Side

Sorting depends on the understanding of citizens, lack of appropriate directions to the citizens regarding sorting

Citizens have no feedback about their efforts in sorting and how much waste they created

Solution

Burba project developed an innovative product to optimize waste management through the use of RFID & LBS technologies, they got it integrated into an intelligent waste container

Intelligent waste container will be able to identify the citizen through a personal RFID card which will be used to open the lid of the container and this data can be used to give feedback to the citizen, the smart container is able to identify items marked with RFID tags.

By these methods a citizen is notified how much waste he created and also whether he separated/sorted the waste accordingly, on the basis of this municipality can create incentive based recycling programs and charge citizens accordingly

In future it is expected that everything will have RFID tags, so when citizen try to dispose of item, RFID can be used to identify type of waste and can help the citizen separating the waste.

Health
(RFID Makes Surgery Safe)

Have you ever heard, that doctor forget towel in a person's stomach after operation, I have heard this numerous times, surgical towels are used either they are placed under the organ to stop bleeding or give better exposure of that organ to the doctor so doctor can operate, sometimes doctor forgets that towel and close the cut.

Actually towels are counted before getting into operating table, dustbin is emptied, each time towels are counted before inserting and removing, but even then can doctors forget them, it is quite a common scene with every 1/3000 to 1/5000 cases, in case of stomach operation it is 1 in 1000/1500.

this is not actually doctor's carelessness, but human error, there is such a mess during operation, this mistake is serious trouble to patients, they might develop puss in that area and severe infection and pain

Solution

IOT(Internet of Things)

is going to help here

In order to solve this problem, surgical towels should be equipped with RFID, so that each towel can be identified, and by installing RFID antennas it is possible to track all the towels and make sure that no towels are missing

Currently because of very high prices surgical towels with integrated RFID are not available in market but it is completely implemented in Munich Germany Isar River University Hospital

Nature Monitoring
(Monna Connected Birds)

Monna plans to launch Europe into global leadership for monitoring nature, it combines technical development for analysis of bird migration, it is based on research and development of bird monitoring system and use that data in scientific, technological and academic field

Aguila Technologies have developed this systems, the tracker developed for Monna relies on a miniaturized high sensitive GNSS/GPS geo positioning technology. The GPS used allows to receive quality signals even when poor satellite coverage and in bad weather conditions.

The long range transmission relies on UNB (Ultra Narrow band) technology, Monna trackers use the sigfox network which allows European coverage

The embedded transmission carried by bird can send data up to 30km.

Monna Project Also Received award in 2013 from the SIAD (Salon International de l' Agriculture Durable)

EKONET Project
UN estimates that more than 50% of people will live in cities, and it is estimated that it will continue to grow, only 3% space is occupied by cities but

City Aware Smart Service
This is actually implemented concept in SANTANDER in Spain

Santander Team is trying to build a smart city, where IOT enabled devices are installed everywhere in the city including inside roads, city has already installed over 12000 sensors across the city to make the city real laboratory in which scientific community can investigate on which companies can develop business application and products and which help citizens in improvement in their quality of life

Key features of converting to smart city is driver knows where parking space is available, so he gets straight to it, reducing traffic on the road, saving fuel and also less emissions, they have sensors panels on the roads which monitor certain gases, c02 levels, humidity and so on

This is already happening few of the cities are already been or getting converted into smart cities

For more info you can visit

http://www.smartsantander.eu/

Careers in IOT

Like in the year 1999, when the internet was new, no one was exactly sure what to do about it, and how to make money from it. Then AdSense and affiliate programs came, and lot of people become millionaires

My career and many people like me, career just happened to us, we didn't plan anything or nothing happened like we planned, i am a commerce graduate, was not sure what to do in life, when I graduated internet was new, but nobody knew how can we benefit economically, I did a computer programming course since I was not getting a job, demand for programmers was so high, that they hired anybody who can just read and write code, then I got a job as a programmer, my salary was very high compared to other programmers because of study and practice I did, I made websites for myself when I was doing job, then got into website business and made money from AdSense and affiliate programmers, it is not like since I was a little boy, I always wanted to be an affiliate marketer or make money showing AdSense ads ☺, I have to constantly update with technologies to make money, since the landscape was changing very fast. I have to update or risk being left behind. I took opportunities as they came.

The reason we need little bit of planning to be better prepared for the challenges, some opportunities or technologies take time to learn, so by anticipating we invest our time in gaining new skills which can be beneficial to us in the future.

LOT of things started as something else but ended up something else; YouTube was started as a dating site, but end up being video channel where people share videos. Key is to get started as soon as you can and then world guides you where to go.

Technology can bring sudden disruption, your career may simply vanish, when 3d printers will be standard for production, many skilled factory workers will lose job, their career will simply vanish,

One thing I will like to tell, don't totally believe to investment/ financial advisors advice, they just predict the future on the basis of past data, which is very irrelevant, future will never be the same as past, and plus they charge you fees for their wrong advice, learn little bit of economics and stock market and invest on your own. The reason these financial advisors and investment company made money is by using a bubble, they made money without adding any value to the society, when 9/11 happened finance was easily available and at a very low lending rate, these hedge fund and investment companies borrowed those money and used it to push prices of land and everything else, since loan was available easy to anyone without even checking their ability to repay, there was sudden demand for goods which again pushed the prices of everything, that's a long big story, how hedge fund managers, bankers exploited the situation made money, fled the country, and now staying on beaches.

I dislike people who make lot of money without adding any value to the society, they just make money by manipulating the system, and riding the people's greed that money can be doubled in months

Google makes money by easing our everyday lives; Actors singers make money by entertaining us, you seen Bournville chocolate TV commercial, in order to eat that chocolate you must earn it.

Technology Careers are high in demand and well paying, it is also predicted to be so in future, long range career planning in technology is just not practical, just plan ahead for 2-3 years.

Currently companies are very busy connecting devices to each other, but we must understand what problem we are trying to solve, microwave oven connecting to refrigerator and refrigerator connecting to microwave oven is not solving any problem, money can be made in most cases only if we are trying to solve a problem or have a solution for a need.

Understand the need and then come up with a solution which can solve the need in better way

Mainly there are two types of IOT opportunity , consumer IOT or industrial IOT, you can be an industrial IOT expert and can help companies improve their efficiency, productivity, reduce or eliminate waste by automating the process.

Or you can create devices useful for general public, like that motorbike tracking app, health app and make a living out of it.

There is a website which provides online training plus practical's and also provide tools required for those practicals

http://www.axelta.com/AxOnlineIOTBootcamps.php

If you are very new, you can do course on axelta.com

You can also find various courses in http://www.udemy.com , but these courses won't come with the tools required to do practicals

So it is better to get started with axelta.com, and then once you are confident enough you can do your own stuff and buy tools from these other websites

In Spite of being a decade old technology, IOT is still at its infancy level, just like internet was at the year 1997, you can be next Google or amazon of IOT,

There are some problems in IOT in spite of being promising technology it is still not widely used, just like Webrtc, in spite of very cool technology for video and audio communication, very few are actually using it.

Problems & Challenges of IOT implementation are discussed in next chapter

Problems and challenges in IOT

Everything is fine, why I need to change; people are somewhat resistant to change, even if that change can bring significant boost in quality of life, when life is going smooth people don't want to change anything, people are busy with their family and day to day life, getting used to new technology which can improve life sometimes requires a little effort which people are unwilling to put, besides they are various problems in hardware design, antenna size and implementation

No Standard format

during internet revolution, there was somewhat problem of browser wars, but the whole ecosystem had a standard format, 90% of users were using windows pc, so developers had never a problem of running a website on windows pc, or Linux pc or mac pcs,

Problem is complexity of hardware devices, and there is no standardization of hardware devices

IOT devices will need a whole operating system, better computing power to do complex things it needs to do.

Devices need to be very small, plus powerful, and also has to have long lasting battery power or has to have consistent power source

Privacy Issue

Privacy at a risk is here, everything about you, like purchasing habits, your tastes, and even your poop details will be stored in cloud, there was experiment in Europe public toilets, there were sensors in the toilets and the data was analyzed, the experiment was done to test whether government can stop epidemic by analyzing the toilet data, that is can it warn about epidemic and take appropriate measures to curtail it.

Imagine if your toilets are attached with sensors, every day your poop is analyzed, your urine is analyzed for problems and its data is kept in cloud, although this data can be useful in case for your doctor or government, your health data can also be very beneficial for you, to understand about your health, but would you like the world to know what you eat on 15th march 2016, and how was your stomach upset on 17th march 2016 and you had gas problem on 28th march 2016. This is useful data for doctors and to you, to better understand your health but it can bring you embarrassment.

If all the public and private toilets are sensored, it can create data which can be useful for government to track an epidemic and detects health concerns and act accordingly.

Although government can say public toilets data is not personalized, single individual cannot be pinned, but that's bull shit, individual can be easily pin pointed.

According to Ayurveda 90% of health problems start with stomach, that is why all the Ayurveda medicine is targeted to stomach.

Your toilet data can help you improve your health, toilet data can help detect disease, you can easily track what causes your stomach to get upset, when your health problem started from which date, you started to have gas trouble and so on.

But you definitely don't want whole world to know about your gas problem, which can easily be known, because whole of its data is stored in cloud.

When everything about you, your toilet data, your purchasing habits, your call details, your car details and everything is stored in cloud that is privacy concern

That's why amazon echo, does not store data in cloud as of now, since that will be serious privacy violation, since the device is always on listening to conversation

Amazon echo is an amazing device, which has a very bright future you can know more about it on YouTube

https://www.youtube.com/watch?v=KkOCeAtKHlc

Security & Hacking Issues

IOT is relatively very new technology, like windows was very vulnerable during 90s , same is the case here, an IOT device is part of your network, if a single IOT device is compromised then whole of your devices of network can be compromised.

People mostly are common people they are not aware of hacking threats and most people can be easily social engineered into giving their passwords, people wants solution and would not like to learn all about security and social engineering, it's not practical for common people to be master on everything, know details about electronics and programming, it's for guys like us to design and sell totally secure and useful applications.

Many IOT devices will come without password, like you just type admin and password is blank, this is a big flaw from developer's side.

IOT security is a different and huge topic altogether, but I will cover some basic and key points

IOT device is always connected to the internet that makes it accessible & vulnerable from anywhere

Making money in IOT

The biggest question asked is how you will make money from it; standard way is to sell the product and make money from it, but the drawback is as days goes by less and less sales will be made, since the consumer's size is fixed to an extent, once everybody has bought the product there will be no more sales.

Below is the graph which shows sales of the most of the companies

You see this is the story of most of the companies; they launch their product and makes good money at the start but as the years pass on their sales decline.

When I was a kid, television revolution came, everyone was buying television, there were at least 100+ television producing companies, but after just around 10 years, hardly 10 companies remained existed, rest all died, why?, now everybody has already bought the television and they won't need television at least for 10 years. That's why car sales are always declining once you buy a car, you won't need car for another 10 years.

Best way to keep on earning money is subscription based model, where you charge monthly fees on recurring basis that will be very steady stream for company, steady stream of income is necessary for growth and you can plan accordingly. Fluctuating income is extremely bad for planning since it disturbs your priorities that's what happens in sales model, once every possible user has bought your product and there is no more sales, you will be confused and will try everything to push sales, but still sales won't come, since everybody has already bought your product and using it.

Monetization can also be the best source of revenue, for example this is just my idea "You offer a Television on subscription basis to a consumer" and you also get paid for ads seen by the consumer which appears on that television, just like AdSense model, ad revenue is shared by Google and AdSense publishers (owners of the website). This will be beneficial for you since you as a company now have additional source of revenue and for consumers also as they have to pay much less to have a Television at their home.

Even in mobile apps world money is not in selling mobile apps, that's just one time money, money is in push notification, showing ads to your app users.

IOT is still a very new concept and here is chances for you to be billionaire build something which millions people will use and then either you can charge based on subscription model or by showing ads or by doing both. That's how Google and Facebook got rich by showing ads to its users. I myself have earned millions of dollars by showing ads to my website users, I have explained how to start web business and how to make money from it in my eBook "Web Money" it's available on amazon, best way to make money is to build something which is very useful to the society at large and then make money by showing ads to these users, who are using your service.

You can check out my eBook here
Web Money Ebook

Where to find materials for IOT

There are plenty of devices for iot available on websites and they all are web enabled, you don't need to be programmer to program them, but it helps to be programmer, you just needs to give time to it, you can easily build iot things within just few weeks of time invested, depending on the complexity of application you are trying to build, and also your level of understanding of electronics and programming

http://www.sparkfun.com

http://www.adafruit.com

http://www.digikey.com

http://www.mouser.com

http://www.jameco.com

http://www.radioshack.com

http://www.amazon.com

http://www.alibaba.com

Basic Electrical Eng Concepts

here you go now, the technical part, these are some of the basic skills you will require to make iot devices, little bit of engineering.

you will be designing circuits for your iot devices, therefore you need to understand at least basic electronic concepts.

good understanding of mathematics is also essential, since ebooks you are referring for electrical engineering will contain symbols and calculations

that's why i will recommend you go through video series rather than books, since you will be confused when symbols are used and you will have to remember what that symbol is called, in video series symbols are said out loud

learn physics, chemistry, maths, mechanical, maths

http://www.magicmarks.in

learning all these subjects help you in better understanding and the video series is cool and easy to understand, you can take 7 days free trial, and then again sign up with another email id and continue with 7 days free trial

i am no way related to them, but there tutorials have helped me a lot.

you can also learn on youtube, plenty of engineering tutorials available

knowledge of electronic engineering is essential

some basic understanding below

Voltage & Current

the above image best explains voltage current and resistor

Voltage is the energy flowing the circuit, energy per unit charge and the current is the rate of the flow of the charge.

Current is the effect (voltage being the cause). Current cannot flow without Voltage.

every metal has some kind of resistance to the current flow, metal has some vibrating photons when the electrons try to move they get hit on photons and energy is released as a heat.

when the metal is cooled, photons are stable and electrons flow is smooth, some metals at specific point of temperature has zero resistance to the electric flow, they are called super conductor

in short you just need to understand, current resistance is higher when the metal is hot and very less or sometimes zero when the metal is cold.

you must have noticed considerable drop in motorbike and car pickup during hot summers

ohm's law is the most fundamental law of electrical engineering, it's everywhere in electronics world, learn more about ohm's law, in books it will be used as a symbol

ohm's symbol

Basic Circuit Design Example

above image is basic circuit design, here the current flow is shown from positive to negative, but actually it is from negative to positive, conventional electronics use this way, but current flow is from negative to positive

Circuit Design With Resistors

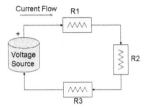

in the above image, the R1, R2, R3 are resistors, they slow down the current flow, when you design your basic circuit board, using breadboard you will be using resistors so that you don't fry up your LED bulbs, when you are learning

Resistors

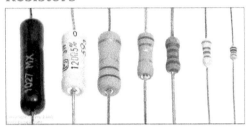

the above image is of resistors, they look like this

BreadBoard

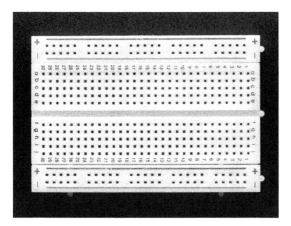

the above image is of breadboard, you will need to practise circuits

you will need this toolkit, if you wanna practise your electrical engineering

while learning you will be using breadboard, so that you can create circuits without soldering, and you can design and redesign your circuits

breadboards are best place to start. That is the real beauty of breadboards– they can house both the simplest circuit as well as very complex circuits.

Basic Tool Kit

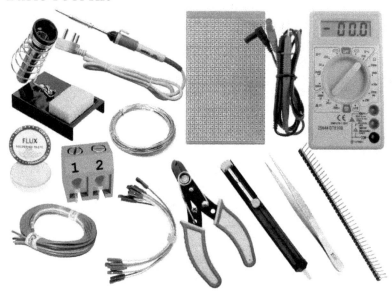

http://www.amazon.in/Technology-Uncorked-Engineers-Soldering-Kit/dp/B01DM5W2UK?ie=UTF8&psc=1&redirect=true&ref_=oh_aui_detailpage_o05_s00

you will also need this toolkit

ATRIM Basic Electronic Component Project Kit

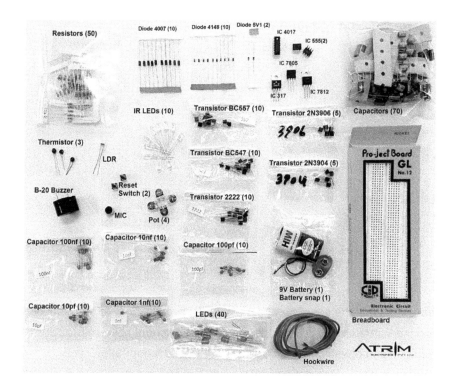

You can buy it from here

http://www.amazon.in/gp/product/B01GCRYYQK/ref=pd_sim_328_4?ie=UTF8&psc=1&refRID=1DRMW00K1KBEZ6P3K7MK

Serial circuit and parallel circuit

Serial Circuit

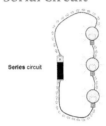

above image is the example of serial circuit, even if the one bulbs stops working entire circuit will fail, people from old school have seen series circuit, like in diwali if one bulb fails, entire decoration fails

parallel circuit

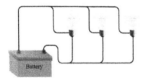

in this circuit even if one or two bulbs fail, circuit is not broken, so entire circuit doesn't fail

Basic Terms used in Circuit Theory

- **AC/DC** Ac means Alternating Current(always changing) , DC means Direct Current (Doesn't change)
- **circuit** is a closed conducting path through which an electrical current either flows or is intended to flow. A circuit consists of active and passive elements.
- **Parameters** are the various elements of an electrical circuit (for example, resistance, capacitance, and inductance).
- **Linear circuit** – a circuit in which the parameters are constant with time, do not change with voltage or current, and obey Ohm's law. In a non-linear circuit the parameters change with voltage and current.
- **passive network** is a one which contains no source of EMF.
- **active network** is a one which contains one or more sources of EMF.
- **bilateral circuit** is one whose properties or characteristics are same in either direction of current. Example: the usual transmission line is bilateral.
- **unilateral circuit** is that circuit in which properties or characteristics change with the direction of operation. Example: a diode rectifier can rectify only in one direction.
- **Node** is a point in a circuit where two or more circuit elements are connected together.
- **Branch** is a part of a network which lies between two nodes.
- **Loop** is a closed path in a circuit in which no element or node is encountered more than once.
- **Mesh** is a loop that contains no other loop within it.

Common laws you should be aware of are
- Ohm's Law
- Kirchhoff's Laws
- Thévenin's Theorem

- Norton's Theorem
- Thévenin and Norton Equivalence
- Superposition Theorem
- Reciprocity Theorem
- Compensation Theorem
- Millman's Theorem
- Joule's Law
- Maximum Power Transfer Theorem
- Star-Delta Transformation
- Delta-Star Transformation

Creating your own iot device

Now that you know about electrical engineering, you must be ready for making your own iot device, lets start

microcontroller & microprocessor

you either will be using microcontroller or microprocessor for your iot device, they both are similar in nature with some differences and usefulness

Microcontrollers are designed to perform specific tasks. Specific means applications where the relationship of input and output is defined. Depending on the input, some processing needs to be done and output is delivered. For example, keyboards, mouse.

Microprocessor find applications where tasks are unspecific like developing software, games, websites, photo editing, creating documents etc. In such cases the relationship between input and output is not defined. They need high amount of resources like RAM, ROM, I/O ports etc.

The clock speed of the Microprocessor is quite high as compared to the microcontroller. Whereas the microcontrollers operate from a few MHz to 30 to 50 MHz, today's microprocessor operate above 1GHz as they perform complex tasks.

microcontroller is lot cheaper than microprocessor

microcontroller cannot be used in place of microprocessor it won't be a good idea, as it will make the application quite costly. Microprocessor cannot be used stand alone. They need other peripherals like RAM, ROM, buffer, I/O ports etc and hence a system designed around a microprocessor is quite costly.

Arduino Board

Now let's Start doing our own sample basic project, we will be using arduino uno device, you can buy that from amazon.com.

when you buy, buy the original, make sure there is a golden mark just besides the USB socket, if it is golden then that's the original, rest clones will have blue, green mark.

best part of arduino is it is open source, you can make your own arduino board by purchasing separate parts of it and then assembling it.

arduino "UNO" has two microcontrollers.

arduino uno has its own details, i will explain some of them, or you can buy ebook about arduino, after you purchased arduino, take a photograph of it from your mobile phone, so that you can enlarge it and see the details

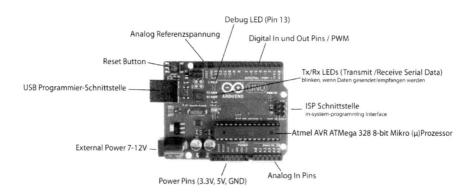

details check out the image of the arduino board, it has some details explained, best thing to do is search for image on google with details of arduino uno board, it will explain, and also take photograph of your arduino board and zoom it to see more details.

it is programmed with bootloader program in the microcontroller memory, it is basic C, you can write c programs and upload it on the microcontroller

look at the usb port in arduino, there you will plug your USB cable and connect it to your computer

Arduino comes with its development IDE, you can download it from

https://www.arduino.cc/

it is very easy to use software with example code in it. in fact it is way too easy to get started, once you connect your arduino board to computer and run the arduino IDE, it will self-select type of board and port connected to it.

the above image shows types of examples available for arduino board, just select any of these and it will load the code needed to it.

now we are going to do a very simple project of blinky, we are going to select if from the examples provided by the software, below is the image how to select example of blinky.

you are going to go into file menu/examples/01 basics/blink

it will load the sample code in the IDE, code will look like this

==== code starts==========

void setup() {

    // initialize digital pin LED_BUILTIN as an output.

      pinMode(LED_BUILTIN, OUTPUT);

}

// the loop function runs over and over again forever

void loop() {

```
    digitalWrite(LED_BUILTIN, HIGH);   // turn the LED on (HIGH
    is the voltage level)  delay(1000);                    // wait for a
    second

    digitalWrite(LED_BUILTIN, LOW);         // turn the LED off
by making the voltage LOW

    delay(1000);                       // wait for a second

}
```

===========code ends==

in the setup function, we are specifying pinmode, that is led light built in the Arduino board, the above code will blink the arduino built in light.

in the loop function, which will be running continuously we are specifying to light it, then wait for 1 second and then again light it.

iam pasting the image, on how you are going to upload it to your board.

here we go

Sketch/Upload

but before uploading sketch/verify/compile to check your code for errors and then upload.

this was your first program a very pretty basic example to get hang on arduino board.

there are only five constructs available to program on arduino boards

- setup()
- loop()
- pinmode()
- digitalwrite()
- delay()

setup is the construct which runs only once.

loop is the construct which continuously runs.

pinmode is the construct which we use to specify input output pins.

digitalwrite is used when we are going to write to a specific port.

delay construct is like sleep in programming.

there are also libraries available for arduino board, which can be used if you have any sensors on the board.

Working with sensor, temperature humidity

now it's time to bring out the breadboard, wires you purchased for iot prototyping

the sensor i used is Sivy DHT11, sensor which i bought it from amazon , it has 3 pins

it looks like this

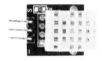

notice the marks at the end of the pin, S and -, we are going to start pining from -

this is how i designed

now erase the program of blinky from your arduino

===== code starts================

```
void setup() {

  // initialize digital pin LED_BUILTIN as an output.



}



// the loop function runs over and over again forever

void loop() {

                // wait for a second

}
```

===== code ends================

have these functions empty and then upload those sketches, done now?

now when you are using breadboard, you need to learn some of the things about breadboard, the line from blue, they are connected vertically, check on the last slot i have put the sensor, and on another i have plugged wires, because they are connected line by line vertically.

temperature sensor has 3 pins, i am starting from negative, negative pin i am connecting through wire to gnd pin on arduino board, and 5 volts pin iam connecting it to the positive pin of the sensor, and A0 pin of arduino board iam connecting it to the middle pin of weather sensor, thats it, its done, check out the image i posted above, how to pin the wires to the sensor and the board, make sure pins are properly inserted and in proper line, so they are in the same flow.

now add the code there, make a sketch(code) to upload to the arduino board

i have uploaded the code and library required on my blog

http://www.aminnagpure.com/2016/06/internet-of-things-ebook-for-free.html

======== code starts here====

#include <dht.h>

#define dht_apin A0 // Analog Pin sensor is connected to

dht DHT;

void setup()

{

  Serial.begin(9600);

  delay(500);//Delay to let system boot

  Serial.println("DHT11 Humidity & temperature Sensor\n\n");

  delay(1000);//Wait before accessing Sensor

}

```
//end "setup()"



void loop()

{

        //Start of Program

        DHT.read11(dht_apin);

      Serial.print("Current humidity = ");

      Serial.print(DHT.humidity);

      Serial.print("%  ");

      Serial.print("temperature = ");

     Serial.print(DHT.temperature);

      Serial.println("C  ");

        delay(5000);//Wait 5 seconds before accessing sensor again.

   //Fastest should be once every two seconds.



}

// end loop()


======================= code ends
here======================================
```

now that you have run the code, error will occur, because you have not added the library

Menu/Sketch/Include Library/Add .Zip Library

iam pasting an image on how to add library to your code file

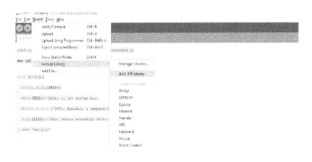

now once you add the library, your code will be working, then upload your code to the arduino board, and voila your work is done here.

to check the results, we need to click on serial monitor, which is at extreme right of the arduino software IDE.

There you will see results, like this

that's great, everything is done and the code is working

now sending data to the cloud

Sending Data to the Cloud

we are going to create simple program in nodejs, which will just post data to the cloud, we are going to use thingspeak cloud services.

i hope you know programming in nodejs, or at least have understanding of it, since i will be providing the code, you just need to know how to use it

i have written ebook on nodejs with koa2, you can download that, just go to amazon.com or .fr,.uk,.in or any related to your country and search for nodejs with koa2 amin nagpure, my ebook will show up.

just download the latest stable version of nodejs

https://nodejs.org/en/

and paste this code, later you can modify it according to your will

and the code i'm pasting below is, name it as "tempupdate.js"

========code starts here==============

```
var slport=require("serialport");

var request=require("request");

var sp=new slport.SerialPort("COM4",

{

        budrate:9600;

        parser:slport.parsers.readline("\n");

});
```

```
sp.on("open", function()

{

sp.on('data', function(data){

        var datajson=JSON.parse(data.toString());


        request({

        url:"https://api.thingspeak.com/update",

        method:"post"

        headers:{

        "x-myserctuser":"mysecretpasswor"

},

        form:{

        field1:JSON.stringify(dataJson.Tempreature);

        field2:JSON.stringify(dataJson.Humidity);

}

},

function(err,response,body){

if (err)

{
```

```
          console.log(err);

}

else{

          console.log(response.statusCode,body);

}

});

});

});
```

=============Code ends here==========================

nodejs is event driven programming language, complex tasks can be easily done with few lines of codes in nodejs.

now your program will post data to the cloud services of thingspeak.

data is posted to the cloud service

https://thingspeak.com/

later you can login and check the data

thanks for reading my ebook, for any errors or issues comment on my blog, i will answer

About Me

Iam Amin b Nagpure, web developer

You can follow me
http://www.aminnagpure.com

Iam also own 2 software companies

Iam a programmer, web developer skilled in asp, asp.net, meteor, node, sql server, Mongodb.

I thank to internet for the all things I got from it, free source code, tutorials and tons of free information, internet also gave me my first job and my current business.

The reason i am writing eBooks and giving lot of stuff for free is because I have learned myself from all the free stuff available on the internet, it's a payback time.

www.ingramcontent.com/pod-product-compliance
Lightning Source LLC
Chambersburg PA
CBHW070900070326
40690CB00009B/1930